# You Are Now Free to Walk with God

Jack Adams

# DEDICATION

To all those who want to know the meaning of this life.
My prayer is that this book would assist you in that
endeavor. All the glory goes to God!

# TABLE OF CONTENTS

# ACKNOWLEDGMENTS

First and foremost, I want to thank God my Father, who loved us so much that he sent his one and only Son, the Lord Jesus, to bring us salvation and eternal life.

Second, I want to thank Jesus our Lord for obeying God the Father, living a sinless life, giving himself as the perfect sacrifice for our sins, and purchasing us with his blood.

Third, I want to thank the Holy Spirit, whom Jesus sent to lead us into a deeper relationship with the Father and his Son.

Fourth, I want to thank my wife of 44 years, who has always stood by my side to encourage me in the things of God. I have truly benefited from her love and faithfulness.

Fifth, I want to thank my daughter, who helps me arrange my thoughts to make my writing more clear, does all my editing, and challenges me on doctrinal points.

# A NOTE FROM THE AUTHOR

The Lord asked me to write this book when I was preaching an outdoor crusade in India.

I had already obeyed the Lord and written a discipleship course, and now he was telling me I needed to put a small book into the hands of new believers the minute they got saved to explain their new birth into God's kingdom.

This book has been written in obedience to that heavenly voice. I envision this book being used for:

- Evangelism—as a tool for someone interested in learning of the kingdom of God

- Churches—to distribute to new believers when they're first born into the kingdom of God

- Believers—so that they can understand what happened to them on the glorious day of their new birth

I believe the greatest weakness in the church today is the failure to disciple Christians, leaving them open to all sorts of pitfalls, bad doctrine, and unnecessary hardships that could be avoided if they had been properly discipled.

This book is an attempt to put solid information into the hands of believers that will help them understand the wonderful, faithful, powerful, and mighty Savior we serve.

All the glory belongs to my Father.

Blessings,

*Jack Adams*

Reverend Jack Adams

# FOREWORD

It is an honor to recommend this book, written by my good friend Jack Adams. Jack is a committed Christian, a Bible teacher, a leader of men, and a good writer! He is a real man of God... he loves Jesus and doesn't care who knows it!

Jack has the heart of a true evangelist, or a messenger of the "good news" of Jesus. When I read this book, it was like talking to Jack. He loves to encourage others!

I'm thankful that the Holy Spirit led Jack Adams to write this book. Surely all believers in Jesus Christ who read it will be thankful.

Pastors and missionaries in many places will also be thankful for this tool. *Let's be thankful together for the writing of this book, and for what is shared inside.*

We should be thankful that the love of Jesus fills the heart of a man so strongly that he must write a book like this.

A book that comes from the Lord, through the heart of a man or woman, is a labor of love. However, *it is still a labor.* It's not easy to write. A book like this one, written with strong dedication to the truth of

God's word, especially so. The writer is not looking for riches or personal fame. He's writing to please the Lord, and help other Christians. ***This was written just for you!***

We should be thankful for the practical way the author shares each lesson. He takes Bible messages and applies them to life in a way we understand. Most Christians don't read the Bible on their own. The main reason they give is: "...I don't understand the Bible."

Understanding is increased by the wisdom of a good teacher who helps others think about things. *A good teacher challenges us to think better* instead of just telling us what to think. And Jack Adams is a good teacher.

We should be thankful for the author's willingness to share personal stories. The writer's own experience helps us see we have hope and a future as a follower of Christ. We can grow. We can become helpers for other believers.

Many times, Bible teachers leave us thinking they're perfect. The truth is, *even the preacher needs the mercy and grace of God.* Even the preacher needs a savior!

We should be thankful that Jack Adams knows the difference between a **relationship** with Jesus, and **religion**. Jack's relationship with Christ is real! It's not based on a system of rituals and traditions. I like the book, because *it delivers what it advertises.*

We should also be thankful that the author uses many Bible verses. Jack uses the Bible to support every lesson in this book. Everything a man writes may be described as either *opinion* or *interpretation*, except when he quotes the Bible. The Bible is God's word. God's Word is our eternal truth. Every word ever spoken or written shall disappear, but not the Bible, God's eternal Word to you and me!

Thank you, Jack, for putting your heart, your experience, your wisdom, and your love for Jesus Christ in this book. *Thanks for not holding back.* Thanks for being honest and bold.

**Believers need the truth, and you have given us the truth.**

*What just happened?* is no doubt a common question people ask after choosing to believe in Jesus Christ. It is also a question the devil asks every time someone is saved! Jack, Thanks for encouraging believers. As you do, many more will be sure to ask the question!

Bishop Curtis Baker
President, Visionaries International

# INTRODUCTION
## You are now free to walk with God: Understanding the salvation experience

This book has been written for three main reasons:

1.  If you have not experienced the wonderful love God has for you, this book thoroughly explains that love and how you can receive it.

2.  If you are a new believer in Christ, this book explains what happened to you when you accepted Jesus Christ as your Lord and Savior.

3.  If you are a believer in Christ, this book will lay a basic foundation in your Christian life to prevent the enemy from deceiving you.

You may be experiencing the overwhelming love of God and the peace of God. You may even be experiencing immense gratitude and relief because all of your sins have been forgiven.

Being born of God is truly a wonderful experience! You are now on the most exciting journey of your life, and it will lead you right into the throne room of God. You will spend the rest of your life learning the things of God.

God told us that the increase of his government will never end. *What does that mean to you and me?* It means that in all of eternity, you will never stop growing in your knowledge of God.

Our little minds do not have the ability to understand these things, but while we are here on earth, God has given us a road map to follow. And that map is the Bible. It contains everything we need for life and godliness through Christ Jesus our Lord. His Holy Spirit will guide you into all truth.

I ask that you continually seek to know him in an intimate way every day of your life. In my 38 years of walking with God, these precepts have served me well: always be thankful, always be grateful, and always be a worshiper, because he has saved us from eternal damnation.

In addition, to start hearing from God, read and study his Word, pray, and stay involved in a good church where you see the joy of the Lord.

Lastly, you must find your fellowship with people who love God, not with people who help you sin.

This book deals with the elementary foundation of what happens to you when you accept Jesus Christ as your Lord and Savior.

The Bible says, "My people are destroyed from lack of knowledge" (Hosea 4:6). *You don't want to be destroyed, do you?* Of course not!

If you know what happened to you spiritually at salvation, then you'll understand how to access God's grace and walk in the things of God.

I should take a minute to inform you that you have been thrown right into the middle of a war. It is imperative to understand that our battle is not against flesh and blood, but against the devil who is the enemy of our souls (Ephesians 6:12).

It is Satan's (the devil's) desire that you go straight to hell, that you do not pass Go, and you do not collect $200. If Satan is unable to stop you from going to heaven, then he implements his alternate plan. And that plan is to make sure you become an ineffective Christian.

You might ask why that is important to him. *Good question!* When you were born into the kingdom of God, you actually gained access to immense power through Jesus Christ. Satan wants to keep you from accessing that power.

God the Father wants you to have a close relationship with him. He wants you to believe his Word, and he wants you to act upon his Word.

Satan knows that if you believe and act upon God's Word, you will become a mighty warrior in God's kingdom. *If Satan can stop you, he will.* He will tell you every lie imaginable to keep you from believing and acting on God's Word.

God did not promise that when you were saved (born again), your problems would be over. You'll still have problems in this life, but you will have God on your side to help you walk through them.

These are just a few things that Jesus promised us:

- Be of good cheer, I have overcome the world (John 16:33)

- I will never leave you nor forsake you (Hebrews 13:5)

- I will be with you always even to the end of the age (Matthew 28:20)

- I give you peace that passes all understanding and it will guard your heart and your mind (Philippians 4:7)

- My Holy Spirit will guide you into all truth (John 16:13)

So even though we continue to walk through this world and experience the problems of this life, we can be assured of our Savior's love and our eternity with him!

# CHAPTER ONE
## The love story begins

To better explain the salvation experience (also called being born again), we'll need to go back to the beginning and lay a basic foundation of how it all started.

In the beginning of creation, God created the heavens and the earth. He then created light and called it "day"; he created water and called it "seas"; he created the dry ground and called it "land"; he created the vegetation and the trees; he created the sun to govern the day, and the stars and moon to govern the night; he created fish and creatures of the sea, and all the birds of the air (Genesis 1:1-23).

On the sixth day, God created all the living creatures that dwell on the land, each according to its kind (Genesis 1:24-25).

"And God saw that it was good" (Genesis 1:25b).

He then created mankind (Genesis 1:27).

**Mankind was the pinnacle of all of God's creation!**

*Then God said, "Let us make mankind in our image, in our likeness, so that they may rule over the fish in the*

*sea and the birds in the sky, over the livestock and all
the wild animals, and over all the creatures that move
along the ground." So God created mankind in his own
image, in the image of God he created them; male and
female he created them (Genesis 1:26-27).*

God called the man he had created "Adam." Prior
to the creation of his helpmate, Adam went around and
named the livestock, the beasts of the field, the birds
of the air, the  fish of the sea, and all the creatures of
the earth because God had given him dominion over
everything on the earth (Genesis 2:19-20).

Then God observed that man was his only creature
that did not have a suitable helpmate:

*The Lord God said, "It is not good for the man to be
alone. I will make a helper suitable for him."*

*Now the Lord God had formed out of the ground
all the wild animals and all the birds in the sky. He
brought them to the man to see what he would name
them; and whatever the man called each living creature,
that was its name. So the man gave names to all the
livestock, the birds in the sky and all the wild animals.*

*But for Adam no suitable helper was found. So the
Lord God caused the man to fall into a deep sleep; and
while he was sleeping, he took one of the man's ribs and
then closed up the place with flesh. Then the Lord God
made a woman from the rib he had taken out of the
man, and he brought her to the man.*

*The man said,*

*"This is now bone of my bones
    and flesh of my flesh;
she shall be called 'woman,'
    for she was taken out of man."*

*That is why a man leaves his father and mother and is united to his wife, and they become one flesh (Genesis 2:18-24).*

Adam named his wife Eve, because "she would become the mother of all the living" (Genesis 3:20.)

Genesis 2:25 tells us that Adam and Eve were both naked and they "felt no shame."

So, we see that mankind was created in the image of God. Adam and Eve lived in the Garden of Eden and had authority over all God's creation. They walked in harmony with God and felt no shame.

## CHAPTER TWO
## **The fall of mankind**

"The Lord God made all kinds of trees grow out of the ground—trees that were pleasing to the eye and good for food. In the middle of the garden were the tree of life and the tree of the knowledge of good and evil" (Genesis 2:9).

All of this was given to mankind to possess and partake of and enjoy. However, God had one requirement:

*And the Lord God commanded the man, 'You are free to eat from any tree in the garden; but you must not eat from the tree of the knowledge of good and evil, for when you eat from it you will certainly die' (Genesis 2:16-17).*

But then the serpent enters the scene:

*Now the serpent was more crafty than any of the wild animals that the Lord God had made. He said to the woman, 'Did God really say, You must not eat from any tree in the garden (Genesis 3:1).*

5

When we're told that we can't have something, it usually becomes even more attractive to us. The serpent got Eve's attention by twisting the truth of God's Word, causing her to desire the forbidden fruit even more.

*"You will not certainly die," the serpent said to the woman. "For God knows that when you eat from it your eyes will be opened, and you will be like God, knowing good and evil" (Genesis 3:4-5).*

It appears that Eve allowed her mind to drift toward the things that the serpent had told her. She might have thought, "Why, of course, I want to be like God". By all appearances, Eve allowed her desire to go unchecked. Eve eventually succumbed to the temptation and ate a piece of fruit from the tree of the knowledge of good and evil.

Immediately, Eve convinced Adam to do the same. Then, feeling separated from God, they became aware of their nakedness and felt shame for the first time. When they heard God walking in the Garden in the cool of the day, they were afraid because of their nakedness (Genesis 3:6-10).

As a consequence of their disobedience, sin entered the world through Adam, and we no longer walk in perfect harmony with God.

"Therefore, just as sin entered the world through one man, and death through sin, and in this way death came to all people, because all sinned" (Romans 5:12).

Some people want to lay all the blame on Adam. Well, the blame did start at the beginning, in the Garden of Eden. Adam blamed Eve for his failures. Eve blamed the serpent for her failures. All of us like to play the blame game, because we don't want to admit that something is our fault. It doesn't matter where temptation comes from, you are ultimately responsible for your own decisions.

Do you think you're different? Let me tell you a story. When my precious daughter was three years old, she loved to drink apple juice. Now, we stored old cooking oil in an apple juice bottle by the stove. One day, my daughter came in from playing outside, and she was hot and thirsty.

"May I have some apple juice?" she asked.

"Just a minute, honey," I replied.

Upon looking in all of the appropriate places, I informed her that we didn't have any apple juice.

"Would you like some water?" I asked her.

"No, I want apple juice!" she angrily replied.

"Honey," I said, "We don't have any."

She pointed to the jar by the stove and said, "Yes, we do—it's right there!"

"That's not apple juice, honey, that's actually old cooking oil."

She and I went round and round for about two minutes, and she was allowing her mind to believe something other than truth from her father. She absolutely refused to believe that the jar by the stove did not contain apple juice.

So, I said, "If you insist, and I can't convince you that I'm telling the truth, I will pour you a glass."

In her conquering, prideful arrogance, she thought she had victoriously won the battle. Because she loved apple juice and was very thirsty, with a triumphant, haughty look in her eyes, she took the glass out of my hand and took a big swig of the cold and dirty cooking oil.

She was devastated by the disgusting taste of the concoction and went on to inform me that I had lied to her. She blamed me for what had happened.

Be careful what you ask for—you just might get it!

If you like playing the blame game, quit it right now! You can lie to yourself, and you can lie to your fellow man, but you cannot lie to God. In God's kingdom, you will be required to take responsibility for your own actions.

The truth is that you and I are no different than Adam.

Romans 3:23 reminds us that "all have sinned and fall short of the glory of God."

# CHAPTER THREE
## God's mercy begins

God, having compassion on his creation, clothed Adam and Eve with garments of animal skin.

*And the Lord God said, "The man has now become like one of us, knowing good and evil. He must not be allowed to reach out his hand and take also from the tree of life and eat, and live forever."*

*So the Lord God banished him from the Garden of Eden to work the ground from which he had been taken.*

*After he drove the man out, he placed on the east side of the Garden of Eden cherubim and a flaming sword flashing back and forth to guard the way to the tree of life (Genesis 3:22-24).*

It didn't take too long for man to become even more wicked:

"The Lord saw how great the wickedness of the human race had become on the earth, and that every inclination of the thoughts of the human heart was only evil all the time" (Genesis 6:5).

If you're willing to look into the depths of your heart, you know the above scripture is true about us too.

In God's great mercy and compassion for mankind, he locked us out of the Garden of Eden to keep us from living forever in a sinful state. Had we eaten of the tree of life after eating of the tree of knowledge of good and evil, we would have been caught in our sinful state throughout eternity.

Concerning having to live forever in a sinful state—let me make a feeble attempt to give you an example of the pain and anguish that we would suffer for all eternity.

Imagine for a minute being a young pregnant woman in the intensity of labor. The baby is stuck in the breech position. You have no one there to comfort you, and you have nothing for the pain.

You are caught in the throes of labor with this unimaginable pain for all eternity with no relief, and the baby never comes.

Or, imagine being a construction worker, and you have just fallen off a ladder. You are lying on the concrete with your bone sticking out of your leg in excruciating pain.

No assistance comes, death escapes you, and you just lie there screaming in pain for all eternity.

If you can't relate to any of these scenarios, take a minute and think about the most fearful, shameful, painful or embarrassing moment in your life, and then imagine experiencing it forever. Only then has your understanding barely been opened to how horrific eternal life without God would be!

Thank God that he graciously locked us out of the Garden of Eden to keep us from eating the tree of life, which would have caused us to live for eternity with the pain of our sin.

We are his creation. He loves us. He doesn't want us to live in eternity locked in our sinful state. He doesn't want us to live eternally separated from him.

- God wants to have complete fellowship with us, but he can't while we are choosing a life of sin

- God doesn't want us to die in our sin and experience total separation from him

- God wants us to partake of the tree of life, but not until we are without sin like he is

# CHAPTER FOUR
## God's plan of redemption begins

"The Lord saw how great the wickedness of the human race had become on the earth, and that every inclination of the thoughts of the human heart was only evil all the time" (Genesis 6:5).

Man was sinful and had advanced to the degree that every inclination of a man's heart was focused on evil. God, who is holy, righteous and without sin, longed to spend time with his creation who was utterly sinful.

Let's examine our own hearts.

You may have convinced yourself that you are a good person. You can lie to your wife; you can lie to your children; you can lie to your friends; you can lie to your boss; and you can even lie to yourself. **But you cannot lie to God!** If you will truly examine your heart, you know that I am speaking the truth.

"Nothing in all creation is hidden from God's sight. Everything is uncovered and laid bare before the eyes of him to whom we must give account" (Hebrews 4:13).

Which of the following apply to you: Are you evil? Are you lustful? Are you selfish? Are you arrogant? Are you a liar? Are you a thief? Are you prideful?

Or, maybe you think God isn't real or that he couldn't love you.

*How do I know that one of the above applies to you?* The Bible makes it clear:

"For all have sinned and fall short of the glory of God" (Romans 3:23).

You might say, "Okay, I do agree with you. So, then, how do I get out of the mess that I'm in?"

Be patient. First, let's see what God requires of us. The Apostle Peter reminds us in 1 Peter 1:16 that God says, "Be holy, because I am holy."

That raises the question: *How do I become holy?*

God gave the Israelites ten commandments to follow (paraphrased from Exodus 20:1-17):

1. You shall have no other gods besides me
2. You shall not make or bow down to graven images
3. You shall not use the Lord's name in vain
4. You shall keep the Sabbath day holy
5. You shall honor your mother and your father
6. You shall not murder
7. You shall not commit adultery
8. You shall not steal
9. You shall not tell a lie against your neighbor

## 10. You shall not desire your neighbor's possessions

*Are you now convinced that it's impossible for us to live up to God's standards?* You might be thinking: "I got it! But, you still haven't told me how to get out of this mess that I'm in."

Let's consult the Bible: "Jesus looked at them and said, 'With man this is impossible, but with God all things are possible'" (Matthew 19:26).

Now, let's examine the Bible and find out what God requires to take away our sinfulness: "In fact, the law requires that nearly everything be cleansed with blood, and without the shedding of blood there is no forgiveness" (Hebrews 9:22).

*What does this mean for you and me?*

It means that all sinned must be paid for. And full payment can only be made by the shedding of blood. So God, in his mercy, instituted the blood sacrifice to cover man's sin. In Old Testament times, the Israelites would sacrifice a lamb without blemish to temporarily atone for their sins so they could approach God, who is holy.

So, in order to follow the requirement detailed in the Old Testament, we would have to sacrifice a lamb to atone for our sins.

You might be thinking: "There is no hope for me— I would be sacrificing a lamb every day of my life, because I sin every day of my life."

The good news about God is that "in his forbearance he had left the sins committed beforehand unpunished—he did it to demonstrate his righteousness at the present time, so as to be just and the one who justifies those who have faith in Jesus" (Romans 3:25b-26).

17

What does that mean for you and me?

God is not saying that you won't be judged for your sins, but he, being rich in mercy, has delayed the time of judgement until your death: "Just as people are destined to die once, and after that to face judgment" (Hebrews 9:27).

*But what if I told you that this God we've been discussing has provided a perfect sacrificial lamb that doesn't just atone for your sins temporarily, but accepts the entire penalty for your sin, forever?*

You might be thinking, "Wow! That would be great, but how do I find this Lamb of God?

# CHAPTER FIVE
## The Son of God appears

"In the beginning was the Word, and the Word was with God, and the Word was God" (John 1:1).

Speaking of Jesus, Isaiah 9:6 says, "For to us a child is born, to us a son is given, and the government will be on his shoulders. And he will be called Wonderful Counselor, Mighty God, Everlasting Father, Prince of Peace."

Speaking of Mary, Matthew 1:23 says, "The virgin will conceive and give birth to a son, and they will call him Immanuel (which means 'God with us')."

The angel Gabriel, speaking directly to Mary in Luke 1:31 says, "You will conceive and give birth to a son, and you are to call him Jesus."

The Apostle John tells us in John 1:14 that "the Word became flesh and made his dwelling among us..."

John the Baptist attests to the truth of Christ's identity in John 1:29: "The next day John saw Jesus coming toward him and said, 'Look, the Lamb of God, who takes away the sin of the world!'"

The previous scriptures are telling you that Jesus was born of a virgin, his father is God, he is the Word of God, and he is the Lamb of God that has come to pay for my sin and yours.

**Man, that's exciting!**

Jesus lived on this earth for about 33 years. During his time on earth, Jesus declared himself to be the Son of God, God in the flesh, the promised Messiah (savior of the world), the gatekeeper, the shepherd of our souls, the only way to God the Father, and the bread of life that came down from heaven.

The Bible also promises that:

- If you believe in Christ, all your sins will be forgiven and washed away (1 John 1:9)

- If you believe in Him, you will be granted eternal life (John 3:16)

- If you believe in Jesus, you will no longer be condemned (Romans 8:1)

- If you believe in Him, you will pass from death to life (John 5:24)

- If you believe in Christ, the written code that opposed you has been canceled and nailed to the cross (Colossians 2:14)

- If you believe in Him, you will become a child of God (John 1:12)

- If you believe in Jesus, nothing in all creation can separate you from the Father's love (Romans 8:38-39)

- If you believe in Christ, your name will be written in the Lamb's book of life (Revelation 13:8)

During Christ's time on earth, he healed the sick, raised the dead, cast out demons, and preached that the Kingdom of God is near. He lived a life free of sin, and willingly walked up Calvary's hill and was crucified. He shed his blood so that we could be redeemed to God. Jesus was the Lamb of God, the perfect sacrifice that allowed our sins to be forgiven, because "without the shedding of blood there is no forgiveness" (Hebrews 9:22).

God who loves us, raised Christ back to life three days after he died, proving that death has no power over Christ (Romans 6:9).

After he was raised to life, Jesus was seen by hundreds of disciples over a forty day period. We have evidence that Jesus has even conquered death!

We no longer have to fear death, nor do we have to die in our sins. So the saying from 1 Corinthians 15:55b is fulfilled: "Where, O death, is your sting?"

"God made him who had no sin to be sin for us, so that in him we might become the righteousness of God" (2 Corinthians 5:21).

*Can you believe it?* You can actually become the righteousness of God in Christ Jesus!

God is not looking for perfect people. That's good news! He's looking for people who will accept the sacrifice of his son (the Lord Jesus) as atonement for their sins.

He knows you will make mistakes, but your mistakes won't disqualify you. God wants you to continue to respond to him. If you respond to him, he will forgive, he will cleanse you, and he will restore you.

**Wow! That is good news!**

# CHAPTER SIX
## The new birth

When you accept Jesus Christ as your Lord and Savior, three things happen:

1. You are born into God's kingdom, and God himself becomes your father

2. All your sins are washed away

3. You receive eternal life

### 1. Being born into God's kingdom

When I was a little boy, I used to stand across the creek in the woods and watch a rich family that seemed to have everything. I longed for the extravagance they seemed to possess.

I couldn't have what they had because I was not part of that family. It didn't matter how good I was. It didn't matter if I accomplished great things. I still would not be part of their family. That rich father still would never be my father. I would always be on the outside looking in.

I wished that I had been born into that family because I knew that if I had, all the extravagance they possessed would be mine as well.

*That's how the Kingdom of God operates.* You can never do enough good things to become part of God's family. You can never pay enough money to become part of God's family. You can never prove yourself righteous enough to become part of God's family.

It's really quite simple: *If you want to be part of God's family you must be born into it.*

The Apostle John records an interaction between Jesus and a member of the Jewish ruling council. The Jewish leader was quizzing Jesus on how to enter the kingdom of God:

> *Jesus replied, "Very truly I tell you, no one can see the kingdom of God unless they are born again."*
>
> *"How can someone be born when they are old?" Nicodemus asked. "Surely they cannot enter a second time into their mother's womb to be born!"*
>
> *Jesus answered, "Very truly I tell you, no one can enter the kingdom of God unless they are born of water and the Spirit. Flesh gives birth to flesh, but the Spirit gives birth to spirit (John 3:3-6)*

The previous scriptures show a difference between the natural kingdom and the spiritual kingdom.

You've already been born in the flesh, and you have a natural father. But God is spirit. You can't see him or touch him. So to be born into God's family, you must be born into the spiritual realm.

God demonstrated how his spiritual kingdom works in this interaction with Mary, the future mother of Christ: "The angel answered, "The Holy Spirit will come on you, and the power of the Most High will overshadow you. So the holy one to be born will be called the Son of God" (Luke 1:35).

Look at Mary's response in verse 38: "I am the Lord's servant... May your word to me be fulfilled."

Matthew 1:18 says, "This is how the birth of Jesus the Messiah came about: His mother Mary was pledged to be married to Joseph, but before they came together, she was found to be pregnant through the Holy Spirit."

Did you notice that Joseph is not the natural father of Jesus?

An angel visits Joseph in Matthew 1:21 and tells him that Mary "will give birth to a son, and you are to give him the name Jesus, because he will save his people from their sins."

Did you notice who the father of Jesus is? Through the Holy Spirit, God is the father of Jesus Christ.

Did you notice that Mary had a willing heart?

Likewise, if you want to be born into God's family, when the Holy Spirit testifies to you that Jesus is the way to heaven, renounce your sins and invite Jesus to dwell in your heart.

*Who wouldn't want God as a father?*

So, flesh gives birth to flesh but the Spirit gives birth to spirit. God is spirit and he wants to place his spirit within you!

The Spirit comes by invitation only—he doesn't use force. You can't become born again by accident, nor are you a child of God until you invite Jesus into your life to be your Lord and Savior.

"Yet to all who did receive him, to those who believed in his name, he gave the right to become children of God—children born not of natural descent, nor of human decision or a husband's will, but born of God" (John 1:12-13).

Wow! *Who wouldn't want to be called a child of God?*

## 2. Having your sins washed away

"For it is written: 'Be holy, because I am holy'" (1 Peter 1:16).

"Be perfect, therefore, as your heavenly Father is perfect" (Matthew 5:48).

You see, God is holy and has never sinned. If you want to be part of God's family, you must be holy and without sin. You already know you can't live life on this earth without sinning. But, it is impossible to enter into God's family unless you are without sin. *Who then can come into God's family?*

"Jesus replied, 'What is impossible with man is possible with God'" (Luke 18:27).

Let's see how God made entering his family possible for mankind.

In the Apostle John's gospel, we read of John the Baptist declaring that Christ is "the Lamb of God, who takes away the sin of the World!" (John 1:29)

We see that God created a way for our sins to be atoned for in the person of Jesus Christ. Our sins have been hung on Jesus, the perfect sacrificial lamb. Because of the perfect sacrifice of Christ, we are able have a relationship with God—our sins no longer have the power to lock us out of God's kingdom.

We can actually be part of God's family. If you choose to accept this perfect sacrifice, not only have you been born into His kingdom, but all of your sins have been washed away. Jesus stood in your place and took your sins upon himself so you could have right standing with God. Wow! *Who wouldn't want their sins washed away?*

### 3. Receiving eternal life

Let's have a closer look at the eternal life we receive at salvation.

Do you remember, back in Genesis 2 that, originally, in the Garden of Eden, God instructed mankind that he could eat from any tree in the garden except from the tree of knowledge of good and evil?

Attention—this shows that man was originally permitted to eat from the tree of life. So, it was God's original intent for us to live forever.

However, we ate from the tree of knowledge of good and evil first.

"And the Lord God said, 'The man has now become like one of us, knowing good and evil. He must not be allowed to reach out his hand and take also from the tree of life and eat, and live forever'" (Genesis 3:22).

Had we afterward eaten of the tree of life, we would have lived forever in our sin. God in his great mercy locked us away from the tree of life by placing cherubim (angelic creatures) with flaming swords to keep us out of the Garden of Eden, thus preventing humanity from living forever in our sin (Genesis 3:23-24).

So, God originally intended for us to live forever, but he didn't want us to live forever while caught in our sin. His original intent has not changed!

"His intent was that now, through the church, the manifold wisdom of God should be made known to the rulers and authorities in the heavenly realms, according to his eternal purpose that he accomplished in Christ Jesus our Lord" (Ephesians 3:10-11).

God's purpose for our eternal life is clear in John 3:16 when Jesus says: "For God so loved the world that he gave his one and only Son, that whoever believes in him shall not perish but have eternal life."

What did Jesus say? That's right, he said if we believe in him, we will receive eternal life!

"Jesus answered, 'I am the way and the truth and the life. No one comes to the Father except through me'" (John 14:6).

Where does eternal life come from? It comes from Jesus Christ, and all those who partake of him will be granted eternal life.

Wow! *Who doesn't want to live forever with God?*
So, let's review:

1.  By accepting Jesus (the Son of God) we are born into God's kingdom.

2.  By accepting Jesus (the Lamb of God) our sin is removed forever.

3.  By accepting Jesus (the Life) we receive eternal life with God.

### It's all about your decision

God is perfect and holy, and he created mankind in his own image. He didn't create robots. You have the right to choose a life with God or a life without God.

You cannot have perfect love unless you have the ability to choose it.

"But God demonstrates his own love for us in this: While we were still sinners, Christ died for us" (Romans 5:8).

The choice belongs to you. God won't force you to love him.

*Love is a decision!*

You can't make your fiancée love you. You can only immerse her in your love and hope she responds. It's no different in God's kingdom.

If you want God's love, you must accept it. When you accept Jesus Christ as your Lord and Savior, God himself will become a father to you, and he will guide you through this life by His Holy Spirit.

Here it is—God has loved you so much that he gave his only Son that all those who believe in Him would receive eternal life. God loves his creation. God desires that all of us be saved (1 Timothy 2:4). But you are free to make your own decision.

If you repeatedly say to God, "I don't need you—I reject your love," then when death comes knocking at your door, and you stand in front of God, you will be rejected as well. He loves you. *Will you respond to that love?*

Make no mistake about it, every decision in life carries a consequence:

- If you choose to reject Jesus, you're choosing to reject God's one and only Son, sent so you could be born into God's family.

- If you choose to reject Jesus, you're choosing to reject the Lamb of God who takes away the sin of the world.

- If you choose to reject Jesus, you're rejecting "the Life" who gives you eternal life with God.

The Apostle Peter declares in Acts 4:12 that "salvation is found in no one else, for there is no other name under heaven given to mankind by which we must be saved."

Jesus tells his disciples: "I am the way and the truth and the life. No one comes to the Father except through me" (John 14:6).

So, here is the question: Is the Holy Spirit dealing with your heart? Do you want to be part of God's family? Do you want to have your sins washed away? If so, then say yes to God's Holy Spirit, and you will be born into God's eternal kingdom.

"For God so loved the world that he gave his one and only Son, that whoever believes in him shall not perish but have eternal life" (John 3:16).

If you haven't done it yet, are you ready to receive Jesus Christ as your Lord and Savior?

**Pray with me:** *Dear God, I'm ready for a new life. I want to be your child. I want my sins to be washed away. I want you to be my father. I want to be born into your eternal kingdom. I believe that Jesus died for my sins—past, present and future. I believe he was raised to life again to show his victory over death. I accept Jesus as my Lord and Savior. I pledge to live for you from this day forward. In the name of Jesus, Amen!*

If you prayed this prayer and meant it, the Bible says you have been born again! You are now part of God's family, and all of your sins have been washed away. You have been granted eternal life with God.

You are now reconciled to God, and you have passed from death into life. You were once condemned, but now you have found favor with God because you believe in his one and only Son.

So now you are born into a spiritual family. God is without sin. Jesus never sinned. And now you are of the same lineage.

Within your spiritual man, you are without sin!

"Flesh gives birth to flesh, but the Spirit gives birth to spirit" (John 3:6).

You have a natural man and a spiritual man. Your spiritual man born to God is without sin and cannot sin, and he cries out to his Daddy in heaven day and night to spend time with him. The natural man, your flesh, can and will sin. However, just because your flesh still has the capacity to sin, this doesn't give you a license to sin. Remember, when you accepted Jesus Christ as you Lord and Savior, you made a vow to God to have a clean conscience toward him.

Whenever you feel unworthy to be called God's child, you can jump up in your Daddy's lap and ask for his help when you need it.

You might ask: "Why do I have the right ask for God's help?" Good question! Because, God is your daddy, just as we read in John 1:12: "Yet to all who did receive him, to those who believed in his name, he gave the right to become children of God."

God is the perfect Father, and he won't turn you away when you seek his help.

# CHAPTER SEVEN
## It is finished!

While Jesus was hanging on the cross with nails in his hands and feet, he became thirsty. Those nearby lifted a sponge to his lips that had been soaked in wine vinegar.

"When he had received the drink, Jesus said, 'It is finished.' With that, he bowed his head and gave up his spirit" (John 19:30).

What does that mean to you and me? Jesus paid the price. An innocent man was crucified for our sins. You are not innocent. Even after you become a child of God, your righteous acts will still fall short of God's righteousness. So, you might as well accept what Jesus has done for you.

When the disciples asked how they should do the work of God, Jesus made a profound statement: "The work of God is this: to believe in the one he has sent" (John 6:29).

That is why the Apostle Paul wrote in Romans 1:16-17, "For I am not ashamed of the gospel, because it is the power of God that brings salvation to everyone who believes: first to the Jew, then to the Gentile. For in the gospel the righteousness of God is revealed—a righteousness that is by faith from first to last, just as it is written: 'The righteous will live by faith.'"

Romans 3:22-25 says, "This righteousness is given through faith in Jesus Christ to all who believe. There is no difference between Jew and Gentile, for all have sinned and fall short of the glory of God, and all are justified freely by his grace through the redemption that came by Christ Jesus. God presented Christ as a sacrifice of atonement, through the shedding of his blood—to be received by faith. He did this to demonstrate his righteousness, because in his forbearance he had left the sins committed beforehand unpunished."

And again, in Ephesians 2:8-9, we're told, "For it is by grace you have been saved, through faith—and this is not from yourselves, it is the gift of God—not by works, so that no one can boast."

So, what is the Bible telling us? It takes righteousness to start your walk with God, and it takes righteousness to finish your walk with God. And righteousness comes by faith in the finished work of the cross alone and no other way. THAT IS THE GOSPEL!

God made it so easy. Actually, it is so easy that we have a hard time wrapping our head around it. We have a tendency as humans to want to achieve our own righteousness or prove to God that we can be righteous apart from him. It is impossible!

Isaiah 64:6a says, "All of us have become like one who is unclean, and all our righteous acts are like filthy rags."

I hate to pop your bubble, but you didn't win your salvation by your good works, nor can you maintain your salvation by your good works. Unfortunately, you will try to do this over and over again. However, after much failure, you will realize that it's a lot easier just to accept the finished work of the cross. As Jesus said, "It is finished."

Did you notice that he said, "It is finished"? He did not say, "It is *just about* finished" or, "Now that I have granted you payment for your sins, you must live according to the law."

No, that is not how God's kingdom works! This is how it works: "For in the gospel the righteousness of God is revealed—a righteousness that is by faith from first to last, just as it is written: 'The righteous will live by faith'" (Romans 1:17).

If Satan can get you to believe any of the following, then he knows you'll become ineffective in God's kingdom:

- ▪ I am a great Christian—just look at my righteous acts.
- ▪ I can maintain my Christianity by my good works.
- ▪ I must never sin again, or I will lose my salvation.
- ▪ I have sinned too greatly to come back to God.

These are common lies circulated by the devil to trip you up. You see, if you walk according to, or believe, any of these lies, you may begin to believe that your righteousness depends on *your good conduct* instead of in *what Jesus has already done.*

If you believe your righteousness depends on you, you are on the road to becoming a hypocrite, and now you may actually start to believe that you are better than others by the way you conduct your life.

Guess what? If you believe your salvation depends upon you instead of on the finished work of Jesus, then you will stumble. You will fall into sin! And Satan will temporarily shipwreck your walk with God.

Once God has cleaned you up a little bit, it's very easy to become arrogant and think that you've done something great. You haven't done anything great! You just allowed God to change you.

The belief that you have attained righteousness through your good works is generally referred to as a "Pharisaical spirit," named after the religious leaders who opposed Jesus.

Remember when you became a teenager and you thought you knew everything, and everyone else in authority over you was just stupid? As the years went by, you came to realize that the individuals helping to guide you were not so dumb after all. In fact, they had a lot of wisdom to speak into your life.

Of course, we've all had acquaintances that never grew out of that mentality. Even if you try to reason with them, they just don't get it. We don't want to be those people. The Pharisee mentality is a stench in God's nostrils.

"For I tell you that unless your righteousness surpasses that of the Pharisees and the teachers of the law, you will certainly not enter the kingdom of heaven" (Matthew 5:20).

Jesus just flat out tells us that we can't enter the kingdom of Heaven unless we're more righteous than the Pharisees.

A little background would be helpful here. The Pharisees knew the Pentateuch (the first five books of the Old Testament) backwards and forwards, but when the Word of God (Jesus) was standing in front of them, they did not recognize him.

You see, in their arrogance, the Pharisees believed their righteousness came from their vast knowledge of the Old Testament and their vain attempts to portray to God and to the people that they were without sin. Jesus, the one without sin, exposed their wickedness.

We must just accept the sacrifice of Jesus on the cross.

You see, it's not about how many great things you've learned, and it's not about how holy you walk with God. It's about Him (Jesus). He paid the price. He defeated all the demons of hell. We need to learn to rest in the finished work of the cross.

Either the blood of Jesus was good enough to take away the sins of the world, or it wasn't.

## No condemnation in Christ

"For God did not send his Son into the world to condemn the world, but to save the world through him. Whoever believes in him is not condemned, but whoever does not believe stands condemned already because they have not believed in the name of God's one and only Son" (John 3:17-18)

"Therefore, there is now no condemnation for those who are in Christ Jesus" (Romans 8:1).

Because of your faith in Jesus, you are no longer condemned!

"For it is by grace you have been saved, through faith—and this is not from yourselves, it is the gift of God—not by works, so that no one can boast" (Ephesians 2:8-9).

We see here that the Apostle Paul makes it clear that there's no room for boasting in yourself.

- Self-righteousness is arrogance in front of God. It causes people that are seeking God to turn away from him.

- Self-righteousness is pride, and God resists the proud, but gives grace to the humble.

- Self-righteousness is saying, "I don't need a Savior for my sins anymore. I can do it myself." It will ultimately cause you to stumble and fall away from God.

*It is finished because of what Jesus has done!*

The reason you need to rely on the finished work of Christ is that you will fall short of God's glory. And the devil will accuse you.

It's imperative that you know how to access God's grace.

"If we confess our sins, he is faithful and just and will forgive us our sins and purify us from all unrighteousness" (1 John 1:9).

*I'm letting you know that the only way to successfully walk with God is by accepting the finished work of the cross.*

You see, the one who has the power to condemn you to hell is now your biggest cheerleader!

The Bible says that Jesus is standing at the right hand of the Father interceding on your behalf (praying for you) (Romans 8:34).

When is it time to run to God?

- Anytime, because he loves to spend time with his child.
- Anytime you need your daddy's love.
- Anytime you feel you have disappointed him.
- Anytime you know you have sinned.
- Anytime you realize that you have been a hypocrite.
- Anytime you are hurting, sad, or lonely.

Because of what Jesus has done, you can crawl up into your daddy's lap at any time and let him love you, or simply ask for help if you're struggling.

"Let us then approach God's throne of grace with confidence, so that we may receive mercy and find grace to help us in our time of need" (Hebrews 4:16).

"Cast all your anxiety on him because he cares for you" (1 Peter 5:7).

Once you have received Jesus, there are a few things you should know:

- He will never leave you, nor forsake you (Hebrews 13:5)
- He will be with you always, even to the end of the age (Matthew 28:20)
- His sheep listen to his voice; he knows them and the follow him (John 10:27)
- None of his sheep will perish; no one can snatch them from his hand (John 10:28)

# CHAPTER EIGHT
## Final exhortations

It's real simple: God is now your Father, and he's the perfect father. He'll never leave you nor forsake you. He only wants what's best for your life. And he wants to have an ongoing relationship with his sons or daughters. He didn't promise you an easy life, but he did promise that he'd always be with you.

You may not have had a good father on earth, and if that's your story, I'm sorry.

Nothing changes the nature of your Father in heaven. He will love you, he will care for you, and he will require you to grow and mature in his kingdom, because he is the perfect father.

- Being a Christian is the easiest thing you'll ever do because Jesus has provided everything you need for life and godliness—just accept his finished work.

- Being a Christian is the hardest thing you'll ever do because your heavenly father will require you to start facing all the ugliness in your life, and a true father disciplines his children.

- Being a Christian is the most wonderful thing you'll ever do, because you have brothers and sisters in Christ all over the world to share your experiences with.

- Being a Christian is the loneliest thing you'll ever do, because you alone will stand before God as he examines the intent of your heart.

People have accused me of suggesting that "you will never be able to leave your life of sin." Others have said I'm suggesting that "it's okay to continue living a life of sin because you are forgiven."

*Nothing could be further from the truth!*

The truth is: You are a new creation. God wants and expects you to act like one.

"Therefore, if anyone is in Christ, the new creation has come: The old has gone, the new is here!" (2 Corinthians 5:17)

"Neither circumcision nor uncircumcision means anything; what counts is the new creation" (Galatians 6:15).

It's all about Jesus—all about being found in him! Anytime we're apart from him, we will fall short of God's glory. You can't successfully walk with God without remaining in Jesus.

To God be the glory.

Amen!

**The ten commandments of being a healthy Christian**

1. God is a God of relationships, a relationship with him first, and then relationships with others—he has not called you to be a loner.

2. Find a good church that preaches and teaches that Jesus is Lord of all.

3. Get discipled—Jesus spent three years teaching his disciples. Get someone to teach you the things of God.

4. Read the Bible daily, starting in the New Testament. Jesus will reveal himself to you.

5. Pray to God daily in the name of Jesus, and spend time in his presence.

6. Always be thankful and grateful for what he has done.

7. Be a worshiper.

8. Share your new faith often.

9. As the Lord convicts you, be quick to repent.

10. Always forgive others, remembering that God has forgiven you.

# ABOUT THE AUTHOR

Reverend Jack Adams has been married for 44 years and has three adult children who have all spent time on the mission field. He has one adult granddaughter who was baptized in 2010 while on a short-term mission trip in Ecuador. Adams also has two young grandsons. *You Are Now Free to Walk with God* is his second book. His first book, *Go Ye*, is a 27-week intensive discipleship course.

Adams was ordained in 1990 by Jesus Hour Ministries. Since 2004, he has served at Tree of Life church in Pflugerville, Texas, in many different capacities, including elder, men's ministry pastor, and missions pastor.

Adams strives to live out his passion as Jesus commanded through Matthew 28:19-20. He's had the pleasure of presenting the gospel in the United States, Mexico, Costa Rica, Honduras, Columbia, Bolivia, Ecuador, Malawi, Botswana, Mozambique, India, Nepal, China, and Myanmar.

He focuses on presenting the gospel at crusades, and on discipleship. Adams believes in equipping the saints to enter the full knowledge of Jesus Christ. His books are available on Amazon.

To schedule Reverend Jack Adams for revivals, speaking engagements, or discipleship training, contact him by email at *2819goye@gmail.com*.